Hardcover
ISBN: 979-8-9869307-0-1
Publisher's Cataloging-in-Publication data
Names: Bloom, Amanda, author.
Title: What If? / by Amanda Bloom
Description: Signed Hardback first edition.
| Lotus Bloom LLC | Akron, OH | 2022.
LCCN: 2022919979 |
ISBN: 979-8-9869307-0-1
Subjects: Children's––Fiction. | Imagination |
Thought Provoking

Library of Congress Control Number: 2022919979
Written by: Amanda Bloom
Edited by: Danielle D. Smith
Copyright © 2022 by Lotus Bloom LLC
All rights reserved.
No portion of this book may be reproduced in any form without written permission from the publisher or author, except as permitted by U.S. copyright law.

Signed First Edition
Visit Authors Website at http://www.flowersbloom.net or follow on Facebook at https://www.facebook.com/bloomsbucketlist or on Instagram Blooms_Bucket_List. Find Podcast streaming options and other links at linktr.ee/flowers_bloom.

Website: https://www.flowersbloom.net
Facebook: https://www.facebook.com/bloomsbucketlist
Instagram: @blooms_bucket_list
Just Bloom w. Amanda: Spotify: https://spoti.fi/3fWXkUy
Apple Music: https://apple.co/3SVML2G
Amazon Music: https://amzn.to/3rQOevo
Youtube: https://bit.ly/3hguPC5

What if I told you the greatest superhero of all,
Is the person you see in the mirror on the wall?

Some of you may smile, some giggle, most doubt,
But let me explain what I'm talking about.

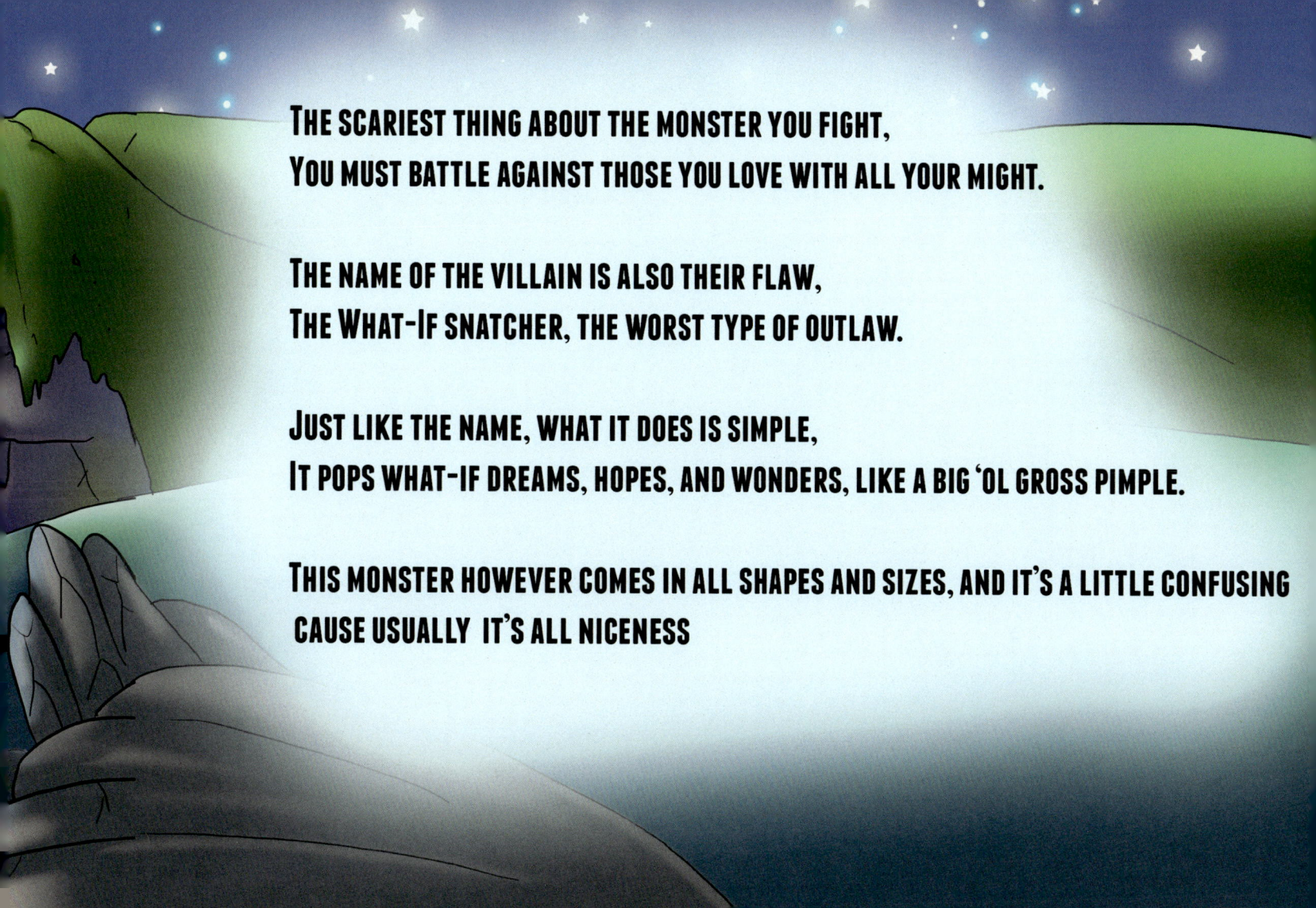

The scariest thing about the monster you fight,
You must battle against those you love with all your might.

The name of the villain is also their flaw,
The What-If snatcher, the worst type of outlaw.

Just like the name, what it does is simple,
It pops what-if dreams, hopes, and wonders, like a big 'ol gross pimple.

This monster however comes in all shapes and sizes, and it's a little confusing cause usually it's all niceness

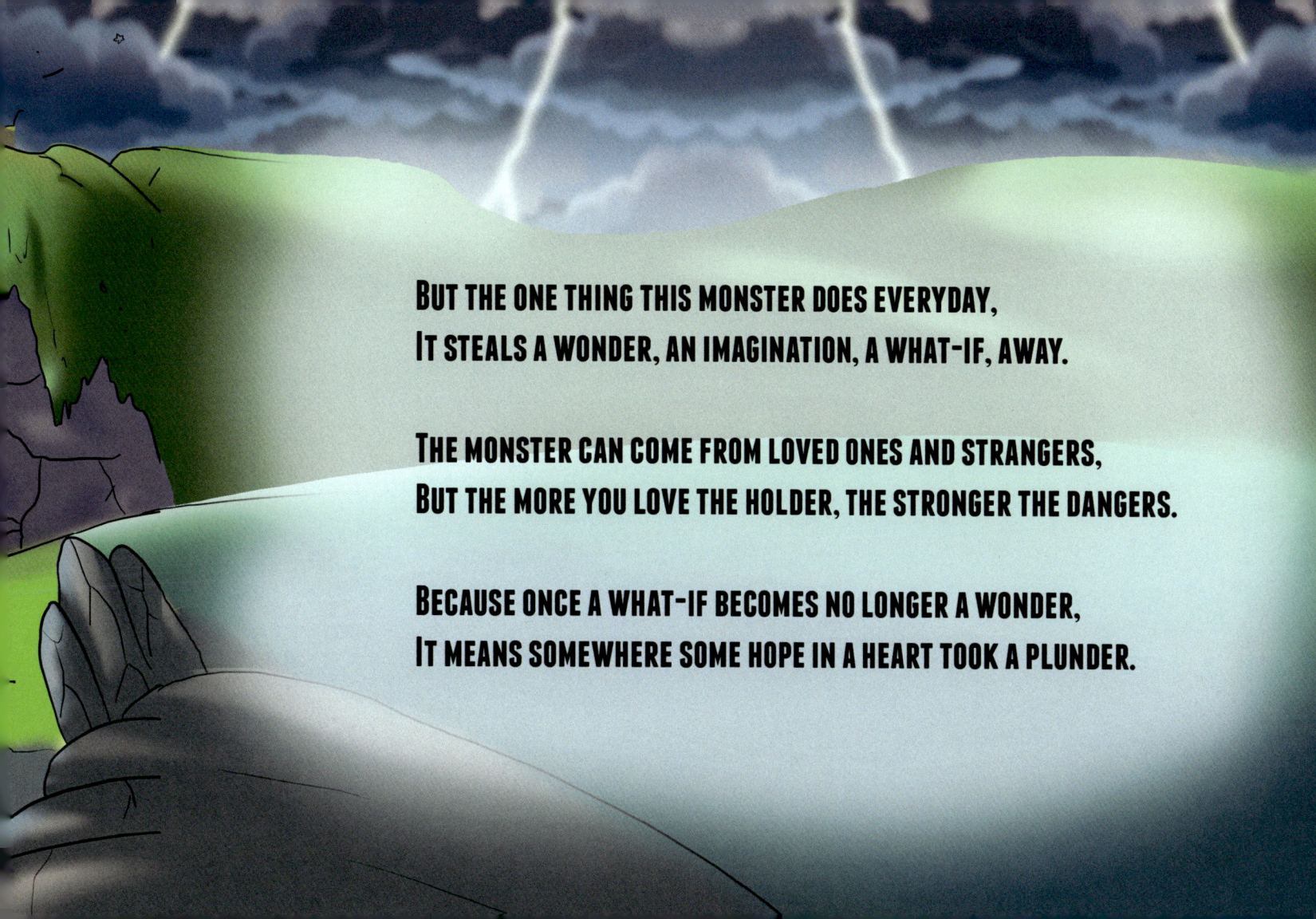

But the one thing this monster does everyday,
It steals a wonder, an imagination, a what-if, away.

The monster can come from loved ones and strangers,
But the more you love the holder, the stronger the dangers.

Because once a what-if becomes no longer a wonder,
It means somewhere some hope in a heart took a plunder.

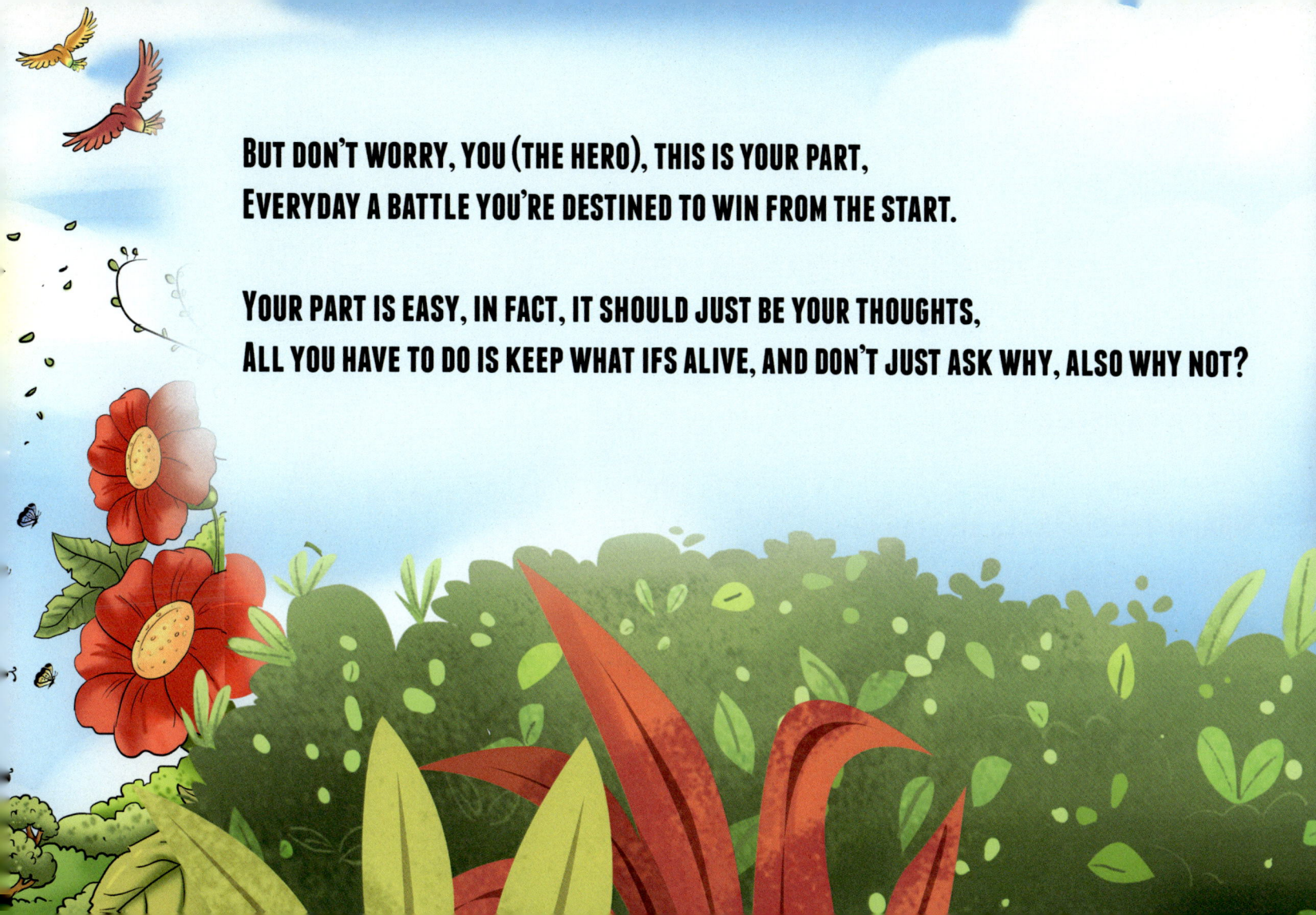

But don't worry, you (the hero), this is your part,
Everyday a battle you're destined to win from the start.

Your part is easy, in fact, it should just be your thoughts,
All you have to do is keep what ifs alive, and don't just ask why, also why not?

What if the grass was blue and the sky was green?
What if Santa Clause was super mean?
What if your foot was attached to your wrist?
What if chicken nuggets didn't exist?

What if the stars all started to fall?
What if kids grew to be 22 feet tall?
What if you had eyes on the back of your head?
What if no one ever decided to slice bread?

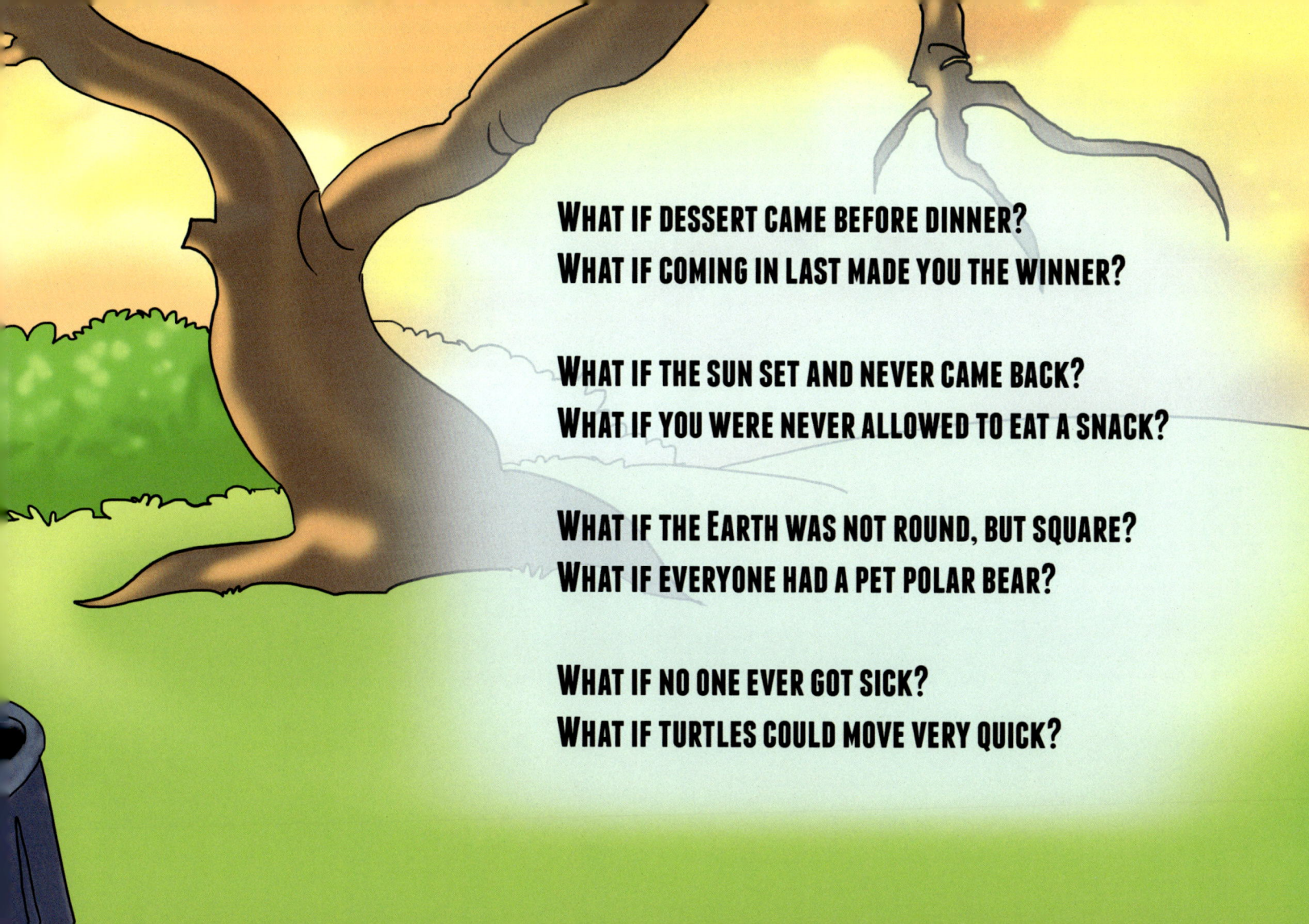

What if dessert came before dinner?
What if coming in last made you the winner?

What if the sun set and never came back?
What if you were never allowed to eat a snack?

What if the Earth was not round, but square?
What if everyone had a pet polar bear?

What if no one ever got sick?
What if turtles could move very quick?

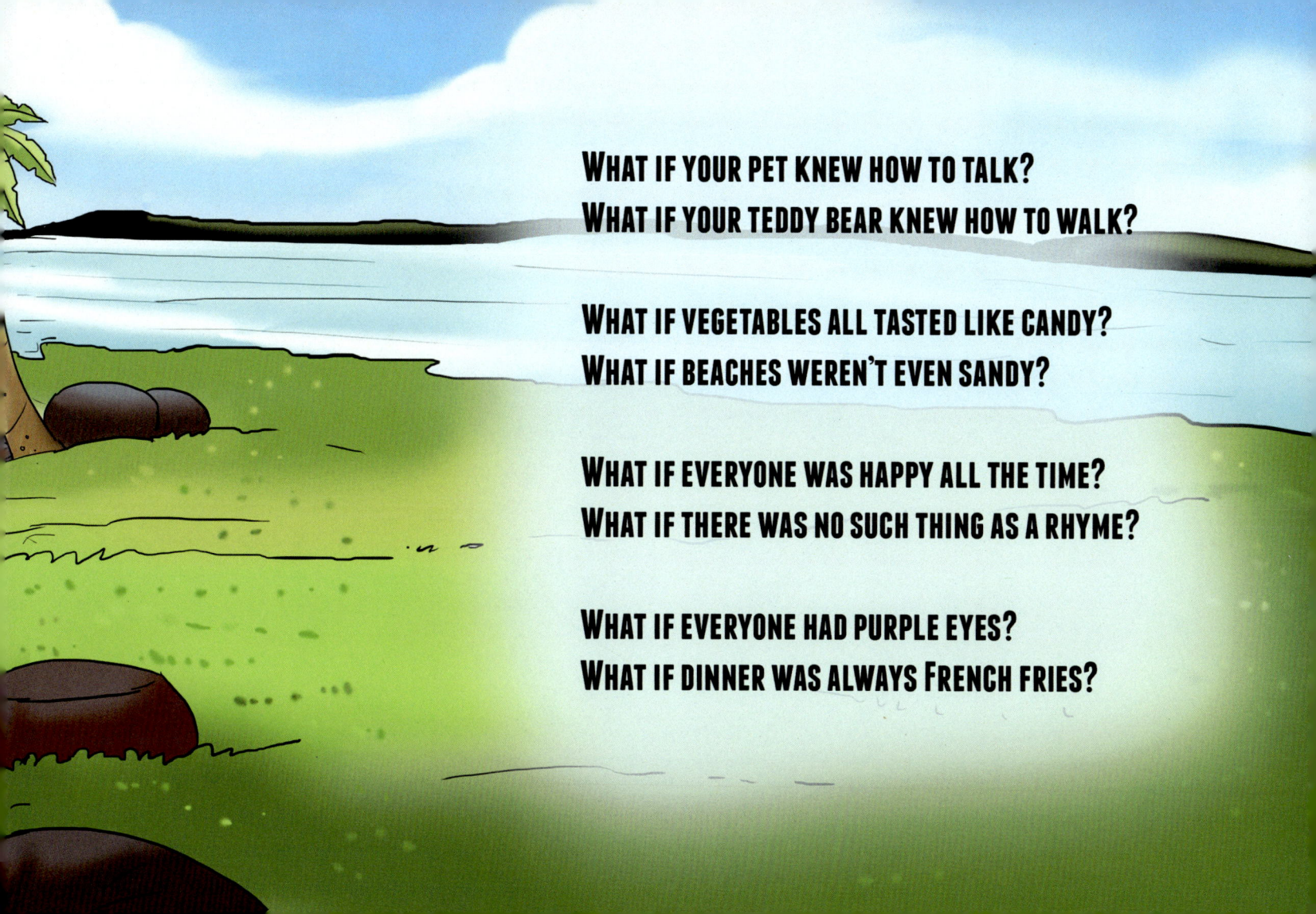

What if your pet knew how to talk?
What if your teddy bear knew how to walk?

What if vegetables all tasted like candy?
What if beaches weren't even sandy?

What if everyone was happy all the time?
What if there was no such thing as a rhyme?

What if everyone had purple eyes?
What if dinner was always French fries?

What if ice cream was healthy for you?
What if you could live in a zoo?

What if it was always light and never dark?
What if only grownups could play at the park?

What if Christmas was in July?
What if pigs were able to fly?

What if no one was ever mean?
What if your room was always clean?

What if toenails were always pink?
What if chocolate milk was the only drink?

What if the snow was made of gummy bears?
What if there were all elevators, no stairs?

What if ants were the size of you and me?
What if money did grow on trees?

What if you could take a vacation to outer space?
What if everyone was all one race?

What if cars had rockets not wheels?
What if bananas grew without peels?

What if your house was made of blocks?
What if there was no such thing as time or clocks?

What if all the oceans were made of Kool-Aid?
What if your memories never fade?

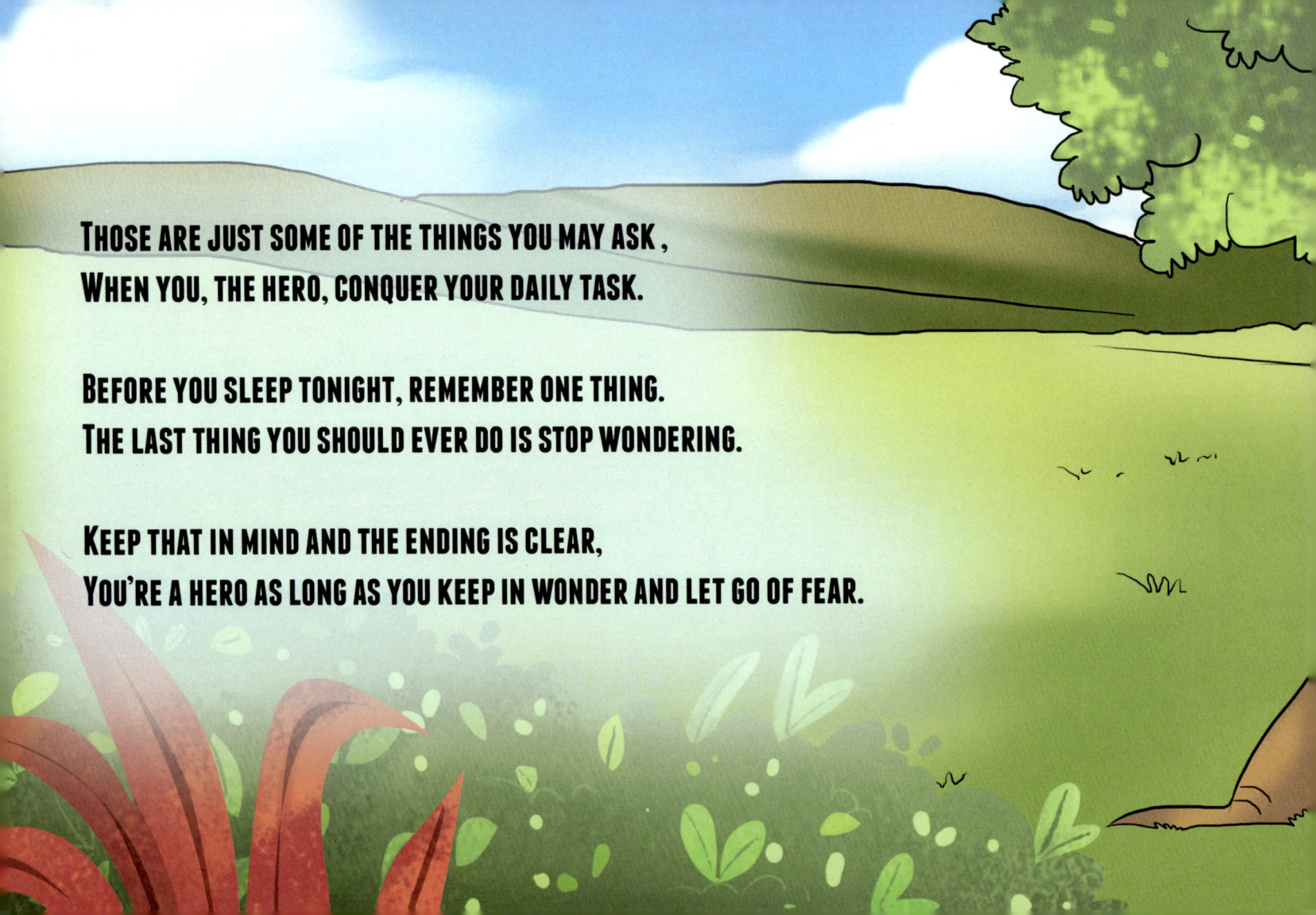

Those are just some of the things you may ask,
When you, the hero, conquer your daily task.

Before you sleep tonight, remember one thing.
The last thing you should ever do is stop wondering.

Keep that in mind and the ending is clear,
You're a hero as long as you keep in wonder and let go of fear.

What if the world was only full of people who ask why and why not? Well me? I think both grown-ups and kids could learn a whole lot!